W9-BZO-543

Dwyane Wade

Revised Edition

By Jeff Savage

AMAZING ATHLETES

Lerner Publications Company • Minneapolis

Text copyright © 2015 by Jeff Savage

All rights reserved. International copyright secured. No part of this book may be reproduced, stored in a retrieval system, or transmitted in any form or by any means—electronic, mechanical, photocopying, recording, or otherwise—without the prior written permission of Lerner Publishing Group, Inc., except for the inclusion of brief quotations in an acknowledged review.

Lerner Publications Company
A division of Lerner Publishing Group, Inc.
241 First Avenue North
Minneapolis, MN 55401 USA

For reading levels and more information, look up this title at www.lernerbooks.com.

Library of Congress Cataloging-in-Publication Data

Savage, Jeff, 1961–
    Dwyane Wade / by Jeff Savage. — Revised edition.
        pages   cm. — (Amazing athletes)
    Includes index.
    ISBN 978–1–4677–1347–4 (pbk. : alk. paper)
    ISBN 978–1–4677–4587–1 (eBook)
    1. Wade, Dwyane, 1982– 2. Basketball players—United States—Biography. I. Title.
  GV884.W36S33 2015
  796.323092—dc23 [B]   2014005593

Manufactured in the United States of America
1 – BP – 7/15/14

TABLE OF CONTENTS

Dwyane *(with the ball)* drives past Manu Ginobili of the San Antonio Spurs.

CHAMPIONS AGAIN

Dwyane Wade put his hands on his knees. Sweat poured down his body as he worked to catch his breath. It had been a long season. But this was no time to slow down. It was Game 7 of the 2013 National Basketball Association

(NBA) Finals. If Dwyane and his teammates could win the game, they would be NBA champions.

The crowd buzzed at AmericanAirlines Arena in Miami. The fans barely sat down as Dwyane and teammate LeBron James poured in basket after basket. They hit **three-point shots**. They made **jumpers** from all around the court. They crushed **slam dunks** when they got near the basket.

LeBron James *(right)* goes up for a basket against Danny Green.

Dwyane takes a shot during the second half of Game 7.

Miami couldn't pull away from the San Antonio Spurs, though. The game was still in doubt with 23 seconds left in the fourth quarter. The Heat had the lead, 94–88.

San Antonio hurried down the court with the ball. Manu Ginobili put up a long three-point shot. Miss! Dwyane grabbed the **rebound**. Danny Green of the Spurs reached out to **foul** Dwyane.

The teams walked to the other end of the court with 16 seconds left in the game. Dwyane had to shoot two **free throws**. If he could sink even one of them, the Spurs would be too far behind to catch up. The Heat would win the game.

The Heat have gone to the playoffs 18 times since the team joined the NBA in 1988.

Dwyane steps up when the game is on the line, and this was one of the biggest games of his life. He had dreamed about moments like these as a child. He calmly sank the first free throw. He missed the second, but it didn't matter. Heat player Shane Battier snatched the rebound, and time ran out. The Heat had won the NBA title!

Dwyane was worn out after the game. "It took everything we had as a team," he said.

"This is the hardest series we ever had to play." The Heat had plenty of time to rest after the Finals. And for the second year in a row, they walked off the court as champions.

Dwyane (right) celebrates with LeBron James (left) after winning the NBA championship.

Dwyane grew up watching NBA legend Michael Jordan of the Chicago Bulls.

ROUGH CHILDHOOD

Dwyane Tyrone Wade Jr. was born January 17, 1982, in Chicago, Illinois. He was the second of two children born to Jolinda and Dwyane Wade Sr. His sister, Tragil, is five years older.

Dwyane's father left home when Dwyane was a baby. The family was very poor. "There were no birthday presents or Christmas presents," said Dwyane. "You just didn't ever ask for what you wanted."

Crooks and gangs roamed the streets around Dwyane's home. When Dwyane was eight, he went to live with his father in a safer neighborhood. Dwyane's dad had a new wife and three other sons. Dwyane felt safer in his new home. "You could be outside at night and not hear gunshots," he said.

Dwyane watched Chicago Bulls basketball games on TV. He studied the moves of superstar Michael Jordan. He dreamed of someday playing in the NBA. "It was my mission as a young kid to overcome being poor," he said.

At Harold L. Richards High School, he played football and basketball. Dwyane struggled in class but tried his best. He knew he needed to improve his grades to play basketball at a top college. His girlfriend, Siohvaughn, helped him study. His teachers helped him prepare too. "We could see how sincere he was," said his coach, Jack Fitzgerald. "We did everything we could to help him."

Dwyane attended Harold L. Richards High School in Oak Lawn, Illinois.

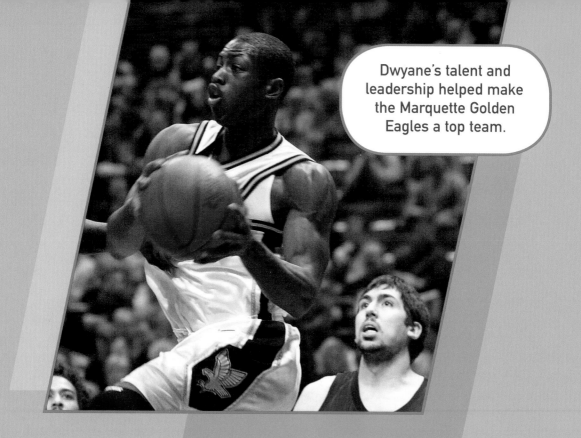

Dwyane's talent and leadership helped make the Marquette Golden Eagles a top team.

MAKING HIS MARK

Dwyane was accepted at Marquette University in Milwaukee, Wisconsin. But he had to work on his grades. He was allowed to practice with the team and wear a uniform for home games. But he was not allowed to play. He had to prove himself in the classroom first.

Siohvaughn moved to Milwaukee to be with him. They got married. Their son, Zaire, was born in early 2002.

Dwyane did well at his studies. The next year he became the team's top **shooting guard**. Dwyane played his best in big games. He scored 35 points against rival DePaul University. When the season ended, he had led the Golden Eagles in nearly every category—scoring, rebounds, **assists**, **steals**, and **blocked shots**. Coach Tom Crean was more impressed with Dwyane as a person. "He has a gift of honesty," said the coach.

Dwyane's coach at Marquette was Tom Crean *(left)*.

Dwyane takes the ball to the hoop.

Dwyane's junior season was even better. He scored more points than any other player in school history. His speed made him nearly impossible to stop. The Golden Eagles were almost unbeatable. In March 2003, Marquette entered the **National Collegiate Athletic Association (NCAA) Tournament** with 23 wins and four losses.

After winning their first two games, the Golden Eagles had a tough game against the University of Pittsburgh Panthers. Dwyane made just one basket in the first half. But with the pressure on, Dwyane scored 22 points. He led the Golden Eagles to a 77–74 victory.

Next, Marquette faced Kentucky. The mighty Wildcats had won their last 26 games. The two teams battled it out, and the Golden Eagles went to halftime with a small lead. Could they finish the job? Dwyane told his teammates in the locker room, "Leave your hearts on the court tonight!"

He backed up his words. Dwyane exploded for 29 points, 11 rebounds, and 11 assists to shock Kentucky. Marquette won 83–69.

Dwyane slams home a dunk to help beat Kentucky at the 2003 NCAA Tournament.

The Golden Eagles had reached the **Final Four**! Their fairy-tale season ended with a loss to the powerful Kansas Jayhawks. Dwyane was an easy choice as a first-team **All-American**.

Dwyane announced that he was skipping his senior year to join the NBA. Before he left Marquette, school officials created the Dwyane

Wade Legacy of Leadership Award. It is given each year to an athlete who shows outstanding character. The first winner of the award? Dwyane Wade.

Dwyane cuts down a piece of net to keep as a reminder of Marquette's win. This is a common practice in basketball.

Dwyane holds up his new Miami Heat jersey at the 2003 NBA Draft. The Miami Heat's Pat Riley holds Dwyane's son, Zaire.

TURNING UP THE HEAT

The 2003 NBA **Draft** was loaded with talented players. LeBron James was the first player picked. Carmelo Anthony went next. Dwyane waited nervously for his name to be called. With the fifth pick in the draft, the Miami Heat chose Dwyane. He had achieved his dream.

Dwyane talks with coach Stan Van Gundy.

Dwyane stood 6 feet 4 inches tall and weighed 210 pounds. He would be one of the smallest players in the league. At practice, the Heat coaches prepared Dwyane for taking on bigger players. Two coaches stood near the basket holding large blocking cushions. Dwyane dribbled toward the hoop. As he jumped, the coaches slammed into him with the cushions, knocking him to the floor. Dwyane learned to shoot as he was falling.

When the season started, Dwyane got knocked down for real. Most times, he got up. Once in a while, he did not. Dwyane missed games with injuries to his hip, foot, and wrist.

When Dwyane did play, he dazzled fans with his moves and cool play. In a game at Toronto, Dwyane hit a jumper at the buzzer to beat the Raptors. One week later, he scored 33 points against the Golden State Warriors. By midseason, he was one of the team's top scorers.

Dwyane looks to pass around Allen Iverson during Dwyane's first NBA season.

Dwyane made about 16 points, four assists, and four rebounds per game. He helped guide the Heat into the playoffs. In Game 1 against the New Orleans Hornets, he hit a 10-foot jumper with 1.3 seconds left to snap a 79–79

tie. In Game 5, he buried a three-pointer to lead his team to another win. Led by Dwyane, the Heat reached the second round of the playoffs before losing to the Indiana Pacers.

Dwyane soars to make a basket during a 2004 playoff game against the Indiana Pacers.

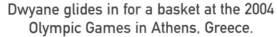
Dwyane glides in for a basket at the 2004 Olympic Games in Athens, Greece.

That summer, Dwyane was selected to play on the US Basketball Team at the 2004 **Olympic Games** in Athens, Greece. He played with other NBA superstars such as Tim Duncan and LeBron James. The US team took on teams from other countries. Dwyane led the US team in steals and was third in assists. The United States finished in third place. Each player was awarded a **bronze medal**.

In 2004, Dwyane teamed up with Shaquille O'Neal *(right)* to make the Heat one of the NBA's best teams.

DYNAMIC DUOS

The Heat traded for Shaquille O'Neal before the start of the 2004–2005 season. Shaq had led the Los Angeles Lakers to three championships. Many people consider him one of the greatest players in NBA history.

In early 2005, the dynamic duo of Dwyane and Shaq led the Heat to the best record in their **conference**. Dwyane was scoring nearly 24 points per game. "Dwyane is on the brink of true greatness," said Heat coach Pat Riley.

In the playoffs, Miami faced the Detroit Pistons for a chance to play in the NBA Finals. The teams each won two of the first four games. Then disaster struck. Dwyane made a quick move and felt a pain in his side. He had pulled a muscle. He left the game and didn't return.

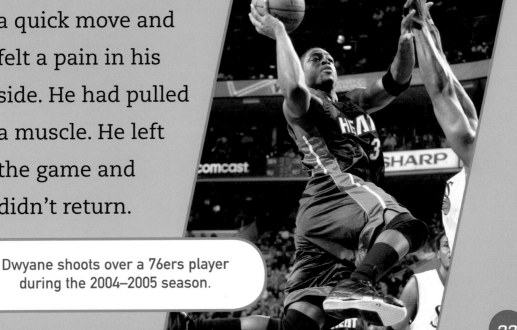

Dwyane shoots over a 76ers player during the 2004–2005 season.

Dwyane cuts through the lane to score a basket against the Detroit Pistons.

Miami held on to win Game 5 before dropping Game 6 with Dwyane on the bench. It would all come down to Game 7. Dwyane was in terrible pain. But he knew his team needed him.

Dwyane played well while often clutching his side in pain. The Heat led by two to start the fourth quarter. But the Pistons won the game, 88–82.

Dwyane's brave play had gotten a lot of

attention. He signed a deal with Converse. The shoe company named a new basketball shoe after him. Dwyane also appeared in print and TV commercials.

The Heat had a slow start to the 2005–2006 season. They got it together for the second half of the year, though. Miami battled through the first three rounds of the playoffs. Then they met the Dallas Mavericks in the NBA Finals. Dallas won the first two games in the series. But the Heat roared back and won the next four games.

Dwyane drives the ball to the basket in a game against the Los Angeles Lakers.

The Heat were NBA champions! Dwyane was named Most Valuable Player (MVP) of the Finals. He gave all the credit to his teammates. "This team was built for the playoffs," he said. But Shaq wanted the world to know what he thought of the team's star shooting guard.

"Wade is the best player ever," Shaq said. Shaq was traded to the Phoenix Suns during the 2007–2008 season. The Heat were still a good team with Dwyane leading the way. Even so, they couldn't get deep into the playoffs. But before the 2010–2011 season, LeBron

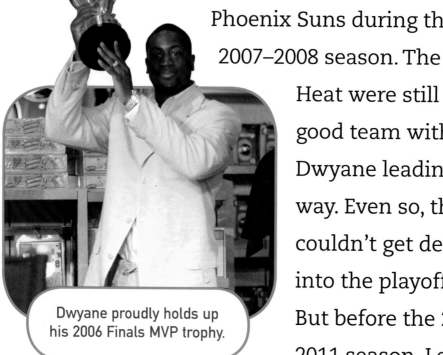

Dwyane proudly holds up his 2006 Finals MVP trophy.

Dwyane *(right)* celebrates with LeBron James *(left)* after a win against the Oklahoma City Thunder.

James joined the team. Miami's new dynamic duo helped bring the team back to the Finals right away. But they lost to the Mavericks.

Expectations were sky high for the team in 2011–2012, and the Heat didn't disappoint. They had one of the best records in the NBA and made it back to the Finals. Miami won three of the first four games against Kevin Durant and the Oklahoma City Thunder. Before the start of Game 5, Dwyane ran back and forth across the court in Miami, waving his arms. He wanted to get the crowd fired up.

Dwyane *(right)* meets some of his fans in Sydney, Australia.

He went on to score 20 points as the Heat won the championship.

Miami won it all again in 2013. Dwyane had become one of the most successful players in NBA history. "I'm living the life I imagined," he said. "Everything I wanted I got."

Selected Career Highlights

2013–2014   Voted to the NBA All-Star Game for the tenth time

2012–2013   Won the NBA Finals with the Miami Heat
Voted to the NBA All-Star Game for the ninth time

2011–2012   Won the NBA Finals with Miami Heat
Voted to the NBA All-Star Game for the eighth time

2010–2011   Voted to the NBA All-Star Game for the seventh time

2009–2010   Voted to the NBA All-Star Game for the sixth time

2008–2009   Voted to the NBA All-Star Game for the fifth time
Led the NBA in points per game (30.2)

2007–2008   Voted to the NBA All-Star Game for the fourth time

2006–2007   Named 2006 Sportsman of the Year by *Sports Illustrated*
Voted to the NBA All-Star Game for the third time

2005–2006   Named NBA Finals MVP
Won the NBA Finals with the Miami Heat
Scored 40 or more points in a regular season game four times
Voted to the NBA All-Star Game for the second time

2004–2005   Named All-NBA Second Team
Won a bronze medal as a member of the 2004 US Olympic Basketball Team

2003–2004   Became the first rookie in four years to be named conference Player of the Week
Selected unanimously to the NBA All-Rookie first team

2002–2003   Set Marquette school record for most points in a season
Led Marquette to their first Final Four appearance in 26 years
Selected as Conference USA Player of the Year
Selected as first-team All-American

2001–2002   Led Marquette in scoring, rebounding, steals, assists, and blocked shots
Selected to the All-Conference USA first team

Glossary

All-American: a college player selected as one of the top in the nation

assists: passes to teammates that help teammates to score baskets

blocked shots: a play in which the ball is knocked away before it reaches the hoop

bronze medal: a medal awarded to the third-place finisher at the Olympics

conference: one of the two groups of teams in the NBA. The groups are the Western Conference and the Eastern Conference.

draft: a yearly event in which professional sports teams take turns choosing new players from a selected group

Final Four: the last four teams competing in the yearly NCAA tournament

foul: to hit or push another player in a way that is against the rules. A player who is fouled often gets to shoot free throws.

free throws: shots taken from behind the free-throw line

jumpers: jump shots, or shots in which the player shoots the ball toward the basket while jumping high in the air

National Collegiate Athletic Association (NCAA) Tournament: a yearly tournament in which 65 college teams compete to decide the national champion

Olympic Games: an event in which athletes from around the world compete in dozens of different sports

rebound: grabbing a missed shot

shooting guard: a player whose job it is to handle and shoot the ball

slam dunks: shots in which a player forcefully slams the ball through the hoop

steals: plays in which the defender takes the ball away from the other team

three-point shots: shots taken from behind the three-point line

Further Reading & Websites

Anderson, Josh. *Miami Heat*. La Jolla, CA: MVP Press, 2013.

Kennedy, Mike, and Mark Stewart. *Swish: The Quest for Basketball's Perfect Shot*. Minneapolis: Millbrook Press, 2009.

Miami Heat Website
http://www.nba.com/heat
The official website of the Heat includes team schedules, news, and profiles of past and current players and coaches.

NBA Website
http://www.nba.com
The NBA's website provides fans with recent news stories, statistics, biographies of players and coaches, and information about games.

The Official Website of Dwyane Wade
http://dwyanewade.com
Learn more about Dwyane's life and career from his official website.

Savage, Jeff. *LeBron James*. Minneapolis: Lerner Publications, 2014.

Sports Illustrated Kids
http://www.sikids.com
The *Sports Illustrated Kids* website covers all sports, including basketball.

LERNER

SOURCE

Expand learning beyond the printed book. Download free, complementary educational resources for this book from our website, www.lernerresource.com.

Index

Photo Acknowledgments

The images in this book are used with the permission of: © BRENDAN SMIALOWSKI/AFP//Getty Images, p. 4; AP Photo/Lynne Sladky, p. 5; AP Photo/Wilfredo Lee, p. 6; AP Photo/El Nuevo Herald, David Santiago, p. 8; © Steven Dunn/Allsport/Getty Images, p. 9; © Howard Ande, p. 11; AP Photo/Morry Gash p. 12; © Craig Jones/Getty Images, p. 13; AP Photo/Darren Hauck p. 14; © Dilip Vishwanat/TSN/Icon SMI, p. 15; © Elsa/Getty Images, p. 16; AP Photo/Wide World Photos, p. 17; © Rick Havner/(The Sporting News)/ZUMA Press, p. 18; © Jon Adams/Icon SMI, p. 19; © Gary Rothstein /Icon SMI, p. 20; © Stuart Hannagan/Getty Images, p. 21; © Paul J. Sutton /Duomo/CORBIS, p. 22; © David Bergman/CORBIS, p. 23; © Marc Serota /Getty Images, p. 25; © Jason Kempin/FilmMagic/Getty Images, p. 26; © David Santiago/Miami Herald/MCT /Getty Images, p. 27; © Ryan Pierse /Getty Images, p. 28; © Gary Hershorn/Reuters/CORBIS, p. 29.

Front cover: © Marc Serota/Getty Images.

Main body text set in Caecilia LT Std 55 Roman 16/28.
Typeface provided by Adobe Systems.